Root English

Book 4

Fantastic Mr. Fox

The Return of Sherlock Holmes

TOEM Books

John Stephen Knodell

ISBN – 978-4-908152-15-3

TOEM Books, Kita 2 Nishi 26, 2-18, Chuo ku,

Sapporo, Japan 0640822

Dedicated to

Yura and Keiyu
&
All those amazing students in Montreal

How to Use the Book

The Roots English series is a content-based textbook that uses authentic readings with grammar, writing, and speaking exercises. While the textbook is rich with grammar exercises, exercises can be used to A) create conversations from the grammar exercises B) test students on the problematic grammar points throughout the book, and C) connect the reading book with sections of the textbook, for example, the making perfect sentences and grammar focus sections.

For classes studying English approximately 3-4 hours a week, try to finish one reading section, one grammar focus/preposition/article exercise, and one writing assignment. Each week, test students on one of the grammar exercises, have a review test of the vocabulary, and always use the textbook as an opportunity to speak with students. In order to prepare for writing essays, debate the topic before giving the assignment for homework.

About the Author

John Stephen Knodell has an M.Ed. in TESOL, and has been an English language teacher for over 20 years. He has taught students from 2 years old to students over 80, from private classes to classes of over 100 students. He currently teaches at a university in Japan.

Table of Contents

Reading

Fantastic Mr. Fox

VOCABULARY TO LEARN

valley, boggis, smothered, dumplings, duck, goose, potbellied, dwarf, shallow end, liver,

mashed, paste, a beastly temper, an orchard, gallons, cleverest, lean, crooks / as soon as,

creep down, rage, lurking, change direction, rip his guts out, delicately

QUESTIONS

1. Where were the 3 farmers' farms?

2. Which farmer ate the most food?

3. Why did one of the farmers always get a stomachache?

4. How thin was farmer Bean?

5. Which farmer do you think was the dumbest?

6. How do we know the children in that area didn't like the farmers?

7. How many people lived in the hole under the big tree?

8. How did Mr. Fox know what to get for dinner?

9. How did the fox not get caught by the farmers?

10. What was the farmers' plan to get the fox?

VOCABULARY TO LEARN

goons, reeks, fumes, poisonous gas, cocky, crouching, gun loaded, no chance, crept,

sniffed, twitched, scent, soft rustling, ears pricked, murky, a glint of, a speck / polished

surface, a flask, took a swig, tenderly, stump, glum, dozed off, soil, sloped, steeply,

panting for breath

QUESTIONS

1. What warning did Mrs. Fox give to her husband before he left?

2. Why was it impossible for Mr. Fox to smell the farmers?

3. What made Mr. Fox stop the first time?

4. How did Mr. Fox know that he was in danger?

5. Where was Mr. Fox's tail?

6. When would the farmers be able to get to the foxes?

7. Which animal can grow back its tail?

8. Why wasn't Mr. Fox so upset?

9. What made Mr. Fox move quickly?

10. Why did Mr. Fox love his wife so much?

VOCABULARY TO LEARN

rose, so...that, to be cross, a swig, give in, porch, a dumpling, as a result, clogged, wax,

muck, deaf, a boil, mechanical, fetch, trotted, brutal looking, toppled, matchstick /

desperate, clanking, too keen to finish,   prowling, dervish, crater, more obstinate

1. How big was the hole now?

2. Why did the farmers get angry at Bean?

3. Why couldn't Bean hear?

4. What was the size of the tractors?

5. How does Dahl describe the tractors?

6. What happened to the Fox's tree?

7. What was happening to the hilltop?

8. Why would Mr. Fox sometimes think they were safe?

9. Why didn't the farmers stop for lunch?

10. What was happening to the farmers?

11. Why did the farmers want to catch the fox even more?

12. Is it important to have wild animals in the world? Why do you think so?

VOCABULARY TO LEARN

switched off, crater, waddling, strung you up, whereupon, a solemn oath, a sickly smile,

scarlet gums / smothered, paste, tender, rich scent, wafted, headlamps, keep watch, laps,

hatchets, armed with, pistols, to creep, a dash for it, desperately, a spark, let them down

QUESTION

1. What is the plot in the story so far?

2. What did the farmers decide not to do?

3. What did the farmers decide not to do?

4. What was their plan to get the foxes?

5. Did the farmers eat something different for supper?

6. Why did the foxes get hungrier?

7. What answer couldn't Mr. and Mrs. Fox give their children?

8. How did the farmers solve the escaping problem?

9. Where did the extra men stay?

10. How did Mr. Fox know the farmers were still there?

VOCABULARY TO LEARN

starving, snapped, a spark, sighed, undefeated, suffering, handle this / disappointment,

raise your hopes, a peep, be sure, wearily, surface, examine, planks, unless, creaked,

cautiously, gap, shriek, prancing, scrambled, a huge shed, teeming with, drinking-trough,

flick, jaws, a feast, in a jiffy, arrangements / bursting in, lack of, starve, spluttered,

plucking, easy as pie

QUESTIONS

1. Summarize chapter 9 in 1 sentence.

2. Why didn't Mr. Fox tell his children where they were going?

3. Why couldn't they know how long it took to dig?

4. How did they know when to stop?

5. What made them all afraid?

6. What "met their eyes"?

7. How did Mr. Fox kill the hens?

8. Where did they go after the hen house?

9. What did Mr. Fox want Mrs. Fox to do?

10. What did Mrs. Fox think when she saw her son?

11. What gave Mrs. Fox new strength?

12. What else did Mr. Fox want to do?

VOCABULARY TO LEARN

badger, peeking, chaos, weasel, we're done for, plump, tease, chickens galore, plenty to go

round / a painful subject, a terrific pace, grinned slyly, blindfold, bull's- eye, gaped, overwhelmed, stored, stacked, grub, sa-liva, ravenously, luscious, overdo it, give the game

away, morsels, loot, a heap

QUESTIONS

1. Why were the foxes so happy?

2. What scared the foxes?

3. Why was Badger starving (hungry)?

4. What did Badger think Mr. Fox was joking about?

5. How long had Badger been lost?

6. What was a painful subject to Mr. Fox?

7. How did Mr. Fox know where he was going?

8. How do we know Mr. Fox was hungry?

9. Why did Mr. Fox only want to pick a few of the ducks, geese, hams…?

10. Why did they take carrots?

VOCABULARY TO LEARN

a tiny bit, gone completely dotty, furry, frump, swipe, respectable, stoop to their level,

here and there, decent, bricks / crumbly, you saucy beast, my private pitch, crept, vast,

damp, gloomy, accustomed to, leaped, tremendous, weak cider, fiery liquor, tilting,

poaching, perched, mind your own business

QUESTIONS

1. What is the main problem in chapter 14?

2. Why was Mr. Fox taking food from the farmers?

3. What didn't Mr. Fox want to do to the farmers?

4. What made them stop digging?

5. Why was the Rat angry?

6. How did Mr. Fox threaten the Rat?

7. Why did they have to be careful in the room?

8. Why did Badger like to drink cider?

9. How good was the cider?

10. Why did the animals freeze?

VOCABULARY TO LEARN

peering, paused, rolling-pin, bound to, strung up, souvenir, stuffed, tucked under, nabbed,

poppycock, bandits / feast, humming, impudent, fellow, the home stretch, swiftly, glide,

bride, groom, hollow, no less than, amid, succulent, belch, a colossal, an entirely new set-

up / famished, keep handy

QUESTIONS

1. Why did the lady go down to the cellar?

2. Why could Mr. Fox hear the sound of the lady's breathing?

3. What do you think the rolling-pin is for?

4. Why did Mr. Bean think the foxes would be escaping that day?

5. Why didn't Mabel take the 3rd bottle?

6. Why did the rat say it wasn't in any danger?

7. What was the theme of the song?

8. How many kinds of animals were in the cave?

9. Why wasn't everyone angry at Mr. Fox?

10. Why did everyone like his plan?

BOOK SUMMARY

Return of the Sherlock Holmes
The Six Napoleons

VOCABULARY TO LEARN

Napoleon, detective, case, silence, ill, mad, busts, madman, crowd, two miles away,

serious, frightened, pieces, noticed, map, quite, empty house

QUESTIONS

1. Why did Holmes like Lestrade's visits?

2. What had somebody been breaking?

3. Where were Dr. Barnicott's busts?

4. Where was the dead man?

5. What had happened to Mr. Harker's bust?

6. When did Mr. Harker hear a scream outside his home?

VOCABULARY TO LEARN

by, carried it away, perhaps, the reason, replied, nearer, the street light, find out why,

until then, not pleased, assistant, useful, rich, poor, tried to, silly story, clearly

QUESTIONS

1. Why didn't the murderer break the bust at the nearest empty house?

2. What did Holmes want to keep?

3. Whose photograph did Holmes show to Morse Hudson?

4. Why did the police arrest Beppo?

5. Who had bought the other 2 busts from the Harding brothers?

Vocabulary to Learn

pleased, clever, reply, motive, murder, a thief, the mafia, punish, broke the rules, facts,

half past ten, walking stick, mustn't, discover, the garden path, waited in silence,

searched, dry blood, unusual

Questions

1. What group did Venucci belong to?

2. Why did Lestrade get angry at Holmes?

3. Why didn't Holmes want to go with Lestrade?

4. How long did they wait until a bad guy appeared?

5. Who attacked the bad man first?

6. How did Mr. brown prepare for the thief?

CHAPTER 7

VOCABULARY TO LEARN

well-known, works of art, servant, just like, cloth, cupboard, proved, immediately, at last,

waned, madman, cases

QUESTIONS

1. How does the reader know that Watson knows Holmes well?

2. How is Mr. Sandeford important to the story?

3. Why did Holmes ask Mr.Sandeford to write his name on the paper?

4. Why did Beppo hide the pearl?

5. Why did Beppo kill Venucci?

6. What was the plot in the story?

7. What was the theme in the story?

SUMMARY

What is the theme in this story?

_____

_____

What is the setting in this story?

_____

What is the plot in this story?

_____

_____

Who are the characters in this story?

_____

_____

What is the atmosphere in this story?

_____

_____

The Norwood Builder

CHAPTER 1

VOCABULARY TO LEARN

cases, selfish, frightened, breathing hard, a lawyer, untidy clothes, fair hair, plenty of

money, suddenly, rang, half an hour, his will, exactly, except, a copy, until

QUESTIONS

1. What was McFarlane's job?

2. Why was Holmes happy when he first talked to McFarlane?

3. What did the police think McFarlane had done?

4. Where did McFarlane sleep the night before?

5. Who does McFarlane live with?

6. Whose name was in Oldacre's will?

7. What did Oldacre ask McFarlane not to do?

8. Where did Holmes want to go first?

9. What did Oldacre ask McFarlane to do?

10. What did McFarlane say when the police took him away?

VOCABULARY TO LEARN

rather surprising, because of, his will, clever, his servant, carelessly, murderer, perhaps,

other motive, not necessary, quite late, returned, facts, unpleasant, discovered, full of

hate, nearest, packets, closed with red wax,   bank book

1. When did Oldacre write his will?

2. Where did Oldacre write his will?

3. When did he write the parts that were hard to read?

4. What is strange to Holmes?

5. Why does Lestrade think that Oldacre was killed?

6. Why did McFarlane's mother refuse to marry Oldacre?

7. Why did Oldacre only have a little money in the bank?

8. How do we know that Oldacre hated the McFarlane family?

9. What does Holmes think will happen to McFarlane?

10. What did a doctor think died in the fire?

VOCABULARY TO LEARN

clearly pleased, reply, thumbprint, proudly, mad, followed, every passage, plenty, start a

fire, the last 2 days, repeated, rude, underneath, clear tome, properly, so proud, refused,

at last, exists, at last, angry silence

QUESTIONS

1. Where, in the hall, was the finger mark?

2. Who found the finger mark?

3. What did the policemen take to the top of the house?

4. What does Sherlock Holmes not like?

5. How many policemen were in the house?

6. How does Holmes know that the finger mark was not there the day before?

7. Where did Oldacre appear from?

8. What did Holmes notice about the passages?

9. Who was going to be "Mr. Cornelius?

10. What did Oldacre burn with the wood?

Summary

What is the theme in this story?

What is the setting in this story?

What is the plot in this story?

Who are the characters in this story?

What is the atmosphere in this story?

The Golden Glasses

VOCABULARY TO LEARN

by the fire, detective, Scotland Yard, doesn't matter, in the country, clever, gardener,

professor, employ, secretary, escape, the study, looks closely, optician, unusually,

mended, catch the train

QUESTIONS

1. What is the feeling of the story?

2. Who was the visitor?

3. Where had he been?

4. Who was dead?

5. Why did the detective think that the case was difficult to solve?

6. How was the person killed?

7. What did the dead person say before dying?

8. How did Holmes know so much about the woman?

VOCABULARY TO LEARN

prints, the only way, weak eyes, keyholes, ordinary, get free, no way out of, notice,

exactly, beard, belong to, cupboard, professor, interested, a large breakfast

QUESTIONS

1. What did Holmes see on the cupboard lock?

2. What was strange about the passage to the professor's room?

3. Why did Holmes think the woman was clever?

4. Why did the woman leave a mark on the lock?

5. What did the professor say was the reason for Smith's death?

6. What did Mrs. Marker say about the professor's meals?

7. What did Holmes think would help in the case?

8. Where is the professor's wife?

VOCABULARY TO LEARN

already, solved, towards, serious, sharp point, her own knife, shelves, cried out,

revolutionaries, prison, offered, permission, packet, embassy, poison, straight, narrow, ash

QUESTIONS

1. Why did Holmes think that the killing of Smith was a mistake?

2. What was the lady's second mistake?

3. What did Holmes do before figuring out the case?

4. What was the lady's second mistake?

5. Why do you think Coram helped the lady?

6. In Russia, what were Anna and her husband?

7. What did Alexis try to do?

8. Who found out where the letters from Alexis were?

9. What did Anna ask Holmes to do?

10. Why did Holmes drop ash on the floor?

11. Why did he knock the box of cigarettes onto the floor?

12. Why do you think Anna took the poison?

SUMMARY

What is the theme in this story?

What is the setting in this story?

What is the plot in this story?

Who are the characters in this story?

What is the atmosphere in this story?

Grammar Focus Section

Grammar Focus 1

*All of the sentences below have mistakes. You must correct the sentences, and make them **PERFECT**.*

1. When I go Korea restaurant, I eat always bibimbap because delicious.

2. She hate to wake earlier because she go to bed lately.

3. In the summer, I play the golf on weekend and it take long time.

4. In the winter is too cold, so I am want to moving in a warmer countries.

5. Mine eyes is good so I need not wearing glasses.

6. I am not happy too much because I don't have money a lot.

7. If a childs behave bad on a restaurant, I feel like to leave right away.

8. My dog tail is short, but am not sure why he tail shorter.

9. I don't know what time is it, so maybe I will going to be late at my job.

10. The most of people in Montreal has good cloth, excepting me.

Grammar Focus 2

All of the sentences below have mistakes. You must correct the sentences, and make them **PERFECT**.

1. He is most nice person I saw in my life.

___

2. Since 9am, I did my homeworks, so now I want to stop to work.

___

3. She didn't play Internet for months, because she is busy too much.

___

4. I use chopstick for eating a breakfast every in the morning.

___

5. I give a email and a plenty of candy to my the best friend.

___

6. My sister think she is good at sing, but she don't.

___

7. I had a lot of pins, but now it's in Korea, so I don't have much.

___

8. We don't have no free times, so we can't take holiday.

___

9. Every big animals are very scary especially if you see ones in safari.

___

10. He buys rarely a great deal of stuffs for his credit card.

___

Grammar Focus 3

All of the sentences below have mistakes. You must correct the sentences, and make them **PERFECT**.

1. Me and he is like each other, so we almost never argue one another.

2. My dad get a many fishes from net because his job was fisherman.

3. I forgot to brought the book, so I goes to home for getting the book.

4. I ride a horse when I was young, but it was little hard to me.

5. None of my book are interested, so I want to go to shop at new books.

6. On weekend, I clean in my room because it look like jungle.

7. I mustn't not every morning drink many glasses of the coffee.

8. I don't like being alone home, so I am pleased for having my dog.

9. She tells me always to study my homework, and I listen her.

10. As soon as I will wash my car, it will get dirt, so I upset.

Grammar Focus 4

All of the sentences below have mistakes. You must correct the sentences, and make them **PERFECT**.

1. I have a beige pants, but I really like that pants.

2. Many of the people in the earth wears the glasses.

3. Buying clothes are bored for me because I am not like shop.

4. Whenever I go to shop, and I prefer to go in the weekend.

5. He can talk Korean because he has lived there few years ago.

6. I enjoy to hear musics while I drive my car, especially in summertime.

7. She yelled to me for of hours because I forgot about meeting her.

8. Yesterday was rainy day, so I stayed in home reading books and drink tea.

9. People who drives fastly often get speed tickets from a police.

10. I left key in the kitchen table, so I ask owner for our house key.

Grammar Focus 5

All of the sentences below have mistakes. You must correct the sentences, and make them **PERFECT**.

1. Take off your shoe and put it in garbage...they smell is terribly.

2. My new, expensive, black, wide television broke up yesterday.

3. Cooking the food is funny to me, but the other people don't eat.

4. Right now, I write this sentences in my computer, and Hana watch tv.

5. While I walked my dog, I slipped in the ice, and fall off the ground.

6. I'm not a rich even I won lottery the last year (I wish).

7. I have a less pen than her, and she have less friends than me.

8. One of my friend wear a makeup everyday, even she go to park.

9. Our class is begin at 4 o'clock, and it last a hour.

10. It was best pencil ever I saw, so I surprised for that.

Grammar Focus 6

All of the sentences below have mistakes. You must correct the sentences, and make them **PERFECT**.

1. I wish I have a brother because my sister still act like baby.

2. I hope I could go to the Boston in several of months.

3. He is tall as me, and we have both same pant size.

4. Next time I catch cold, I stay on my bed and drink a soup.

5. Before I came to here, I met my friend in downtown and we looked a movie.

6. I bit my dog because in accident, I stepped in his tail, so he surprised.

7. I was a car accident when I lived in Korea, but I didn't go hospital.

8. The last week, I went to restaurant with students in this class.

9. I don't want to jump off the window because this room is the 3 floor.

10. She prepares for breakfast every morning, and it take her a long time for her.

Grammar Focus 7

1. At the middle of week, I try taking long walk in the Monkland street.

2. He pick apple for eating it on breakfast.

3. The police is always trying helping people that are at trouble.

4. I went to Netherlands one time of my life, and it was interested.

5. I study myself on the library whenever I am having a test.

6. My shoes are smelling well, so many of people are jealous me.

7. I asked to him to help my car, but he didn't know what is the problem.

8. At the midnight, I heard sound of cat outside of my window, so I close a window.

9. Scared movies is not interesting for me, so I avoid to watch them.

10. I am fear of snake, so I will never going to go to Amazon jungle.

Grammar Focus 8

All of the sentences below have mistakes. You must correct the sentences, and make them **PERFECT**.

1. I like to playing the tennis early in morning.

2. I didn't felt happy in yesterday's night.

3. I bored with watch this movies.

4. I sometime am tired after teach.

5. I have a new, Canadian, cheap, blue car.

6. If I will go to shopping, I buy orange.

7. He don't has some money.

8. On night, I sit at my sofa and watch the TV.

9. Can she has another pieces of pizzas.

10. I breaked mine finger 20 year ago.

Grammar Focus 9

All of the sentences below have mistakes. You must correct the sentences, and make them **PERFECT**.

1. One of friends have nice home.

2. Some of people in world has green eye.

3. Every days, I drink the coffee and eat the bread.

4. Playing piano always is funny to me.

5. I drink never Coke when I waking up.

6. Each students at this class are very smartie.

7. I can't speaking the French very good.

8. He is a old, funny, Korean, tall men.

9. A airplane flew above my home at the afternoon.

10. The China has very long wall called Great Wall of China.

Grammar Focus 10

All of the sentences below have mistakes. You must correct the sentences, and make them **PERFECT**.

11. I am like him because he study hardly.

_____

12. A library in front my home don't open on Monday.

_____

13. Cat and dog can't living with together.

_____

14. I called yesterday to my grandma, and she wasn't home.

_____

15. These table are make from woods.

_____

16. I want buy a gold, expensive, Swiss watches.

_____

17. Before I come in this office, I eat the breakfast every day.

_____

18. Will you come to United States in this summer?

_____

19. I would like teaching in Netherlands because it is so beautiful country.

_____

20. At the first, I can't speak French, so now I could.

_____

Grammar Focus 11

All of the sentences below have mistakes. You must correct the sentences, and make them **PERFECT**.

1. News on TV are very interested for me.

___

2. I have never visit to the Cuba or Han river.

___

3. I eat slow, so some peoples get angry to me.

___

4. I am more big than a elephant.

___

5. She is nicest ladies at this class.

___

6. I am think that soccer funnest sports in world.

___

7. If I am a king, I will bought a castle.

___

8. Last morning, I don't got up early, so I am lately for work.

___

9. Weather in Canada usually is colder than in winter.

___

10. I can't hearing the song. Volume up.

___

Grammar Focus 12

1. First time I went to the TOEM airport, I surprised.

2. Bear lives on caves at mountain.

3. He is as quickly as turtle.

4. If you wants to be good student, study hardly.

5. Next time I go to swimming, I bring a towel.

6. She is tall, Canadian, beautiful, old lady.

7. I watched movie last night at 9pm o'clock.

8. Last week, I have to meet doctor for check-up.

9. I lived in Montreal since 5 year.

10. He go to the school every other weeks.

Grammar Focus 13

All of the sentences below have mistakes. You must correct the sentences, and make them **PERFECT**.

1. Who is a smartest people in yours family?

___

2. What did you eating at lunch yesterday's afternoon?

___

3. Where was you being borned?

___

4. When will you playing the bowling with friend?

___

5. Why do he likes pizza so many?

___

6. Which of pens in the table is your?

___

7. Whose books is onto your bag?

___

8. How often did you studied on the library?

___

9. How long do it takes you to doing your homework?

___

10. How much cups of water do you drank every days?

___

Grammar Focus 14

All of the sentences below have mistakes. You must correct the sentences, and make them **PERFECT**.

1. I drive careful in the winter because roads are danger.

2. They are more smarter they friends because they studied when they was young.

3. Whenever I am being hungry, I ate some foods.

4. I wish I can being more taller.

5. I enjoy to play the cards, but not for the money.

6. He have never ate a chicken in he life.

7. While I walked at school, I was meeting my friend.

8. I don't like old, small, American, ugly television.

9. I don't have no friend who is doctors.

10. Washing clothes are bored in me.

Grammar Focus 15

All of the sentences below have mistakes. You must correct the sentences, and make them **PERFECT**.

1. My sister's and friend is good at the skiing.

_____

2. The man book is so very interested.

_____

3. She might be study at her room yesterday.

_____

4. Will you bought a ice-cream to me?

_____

5. Some bird can't fly on the sky, so they walking or swimming.

_____

6. As soon as I get up today, I talked my friend by internet.

_____

7. If you can't swim in pool, you had to learn fastly.

_____

8. At summer, plenty of boy and girl are study little.

_____

9. I borrowed a pen to Hana because she don't has one.

_____

10. I hope you will had a greatest summer on your life.

_____

49

Prepositions Section

Prepositions 1

Fill in the blank
Write a proper preposition for each sentence. Sometimes, there is more than one answer. Also, prepositions are used in Idioms. These phrasal verbs must be memorized.

1. I agreed _____ you. Living _____ an island would be great.

2. He aimed his gun _____ the bad guy, and shot him _____ the foot.

3. Living _____ a hot country sounds great. I want to move _____ Spain.

4. I argued _____ my sister _____ the telephone _____ an hour.

5. The plane arrived _____ the airport _____ time, so nobody was late _____ their next flight.

6. I asked her _____ a pen, but she didn't hear me. So, I tapped her _____ the shoulder.

7. After he died _____ cancer, his family sold his house _____ $1,000,000.

8. My mom banged _____ a door last week, and now she has a bump _____ her head.

9. When I wake _____ _____ the middle _____ the night, I can't see _____ all.

10. Boxers beat _____ people _____ money, and boxing is exciting _____ watch.

11. Our class begins _____ 4, we study _____ books, and take a break _____ 10 minutes.

12. Once _____ my life, I stood _____ too fast and started to bleed _____ my nose.

13. I like to blow _____ balloons because it is dangerous _____ do that.

14. When I was _____ high school, someone broke _____ my home and stole my mom's jewellery.

15. Please bring a pencil _____ you _____ class. You need to write _____ many things.

Prepositions 2

1. I bought my TV _____ a store _____ sale.

2. My dog hides bones _____ the ground, then digs them _____. He is crazy _____ bones.

3. _____ Sunday night I _____-ate, so Hana called me a pig. I said, "Oink?"

4. I never found _____ who broke _____ my home. There are many bad people _____ the world.

5. Once I laughed _____ my friend and he didn't forgive me _____ that _____ 2 weeks.

6. When I get _____ home after work, I go _____ with my dog.

7. I can't answer this question _____ the least, so I will give _____ trying to figure it _____.

8. When you have makeup _____, you look _____ a star _____ a movie.

9. I heard _____ my sister last week. She got a new job _____ Canada Post.

10. Robbers hide _____ the police because if they get caught, they are put _____ jail.

11. Hana likes to hit me _____ a towel, but I know she is just joking _____.

12. It's windy _____ there, so hold _____ your hat or it will fly _____.

13. This class is too hard _____ me. I can't keep _____.

14. I've never heard _____ that store. I don't know anything _____ it.

15. Are you free _____ Saturday? Do you want to meet me _____ lunch?

Prepositions 3

1. You paid _____ lunch the last time, so this time lunch is _____ me.

2. Have a great trip _____ Cuba. I will go _____ you _____ the airport.

3. Nancy, your friends are leaving _____ a moment. You have to say bye _____ them.

4. I sold my car _____ $10 000. Then I put the money _____ the bank.

5. When I make salad dressing, I always shake _____ the dressing.

6. Why do you always show _____? You aren't that good _____ singing _____ all.

7. The machine is going to blow _____. Shut it _____.

8. Many singers sing _____ love because that is what they are interested _____.

9. Right now, I am sitting _____ my sofa and my computer is _____ my hands.

10. I stayed _____ late last night, so I slept _____, so Hana was angry _____ me.

11. Once, I stole money _____ my mom, so she grounded me _____ a week.

12. Boats sail _____ the Pacific Ocean _____ Vancouver _____ Korea.

13. My nose is _____ my eyes, _____ my mouth and _____ my face.

14. Hana puts hot sauce _____ her pizza and eats it _____ her hands.

15. _____ no time, winter will be here, and we will feel sad _____ that.

Prepositions 4

1. The airplane took _____ _____ the morning and landed _____ Inchon airport _____ Korea.

2. Before going _____ bed, women always take _____ their makeup _____ the bathroom.

3. That food is made _____ me, and is made _____ olive oil _____ Japan.

4. I need to throw _____ my table made _____ wood because it looks run _____.

5. The team won _____ 1 goal, and the winning goal was scored _____ Kaka.

6. Please study _____ the test. Focus _____ pages 17 and 26.

7. I don't like _____ fight _____ people, especially _____ guns.

8. People enjoy jogging _____ rivers because they want to stay _____ shape.

9. I was _____ a race last week, and the winner was always _____ of me.

10. When people live _____ their parents, that is usually hard _____ them.

11. _____ midnight, I don't like to take my dog _____ a walk.

12. When students fool _____ in class, I sometimes kick them _____ _____ the class.

13. I went _____ the kitchen, chopped _____ some vegetables, and made soup.

14. However, the soup tasted _____ old shoe, so I nearly threw _____.

15. I want to get rid _____ my golf clubs. I've had them _____ 2005.

Prepositions 5

1. _____ winter, children always slide _____ hills _____ their free time.

2. _____ an emergency, people call the police _____ help.

3. _____ a highway, if there are no police, I sometimes speed _____.

4. Gum sticks _____ hair, so be careful what you do _____ your gum.

5. I was upset _____ the test because I got a C _____ the test.

6. I studied _____ the test _____ 2 days, but I wasn't prepared _____ the test.

7. I have an old clock, so I need to wind it _____. It was made _____ 1958.

8. When my alarm clock goes _____, I jump _____ _____ bed, and take a shower.

9. If I eat a piece _____ pizza, I can eat it _____ fast. Maybe I am a pig?

10. The ball rolled _____ the table, and my dog chased _____ the ball.

11. When I walk _____ a street, I usually keep my head _____, looking _____ money.

12. I'm not good _____ video games, so I often see the words game _____.

13. I am _____ _____ sugar, so I have to pick some _____.

14. A strange guy walked _____ me _____ my apartment building.

15. The guy got _____ the elevator _____ me, and asked a question _____ me.

Prepositions 6

1. He said, "Which floor do you live _____? I'm looking _____ Steve."

2. I didn't trust him _____ all, so I didn't give an answer _____ his question.

3. We have used this book _____ October. I hope you're having fun _____ it.

4. Airplanes fly _____ the air _____ very fast speeds.

5. I get $5 an hour _____ drive a school bus. Maybe I am _____-paid.

6. I always _____-cook hamburgers, so Hana likes to play hockey _____ the hamburgers.

7. I am fed _____ _____ walking my dog, especially _____ winter mornings.

8. I play golf _____ my friends, and I go to the golf course _____ car.

9. _____ my computer, I cannot make books _____ you, so I am happy _____ my computer.

10. _____ a restaurant, I always start _____ a salad and pay the bill _____ cash.

11. A salad doesn't fill _____ my stomach, but I need vegetables _____ my health.

12. Eating too much oil is bad _____ my heart, so I need to cut _____ _____ oil.

13. Once _____ a while, I go to a casino _____ $100 and try to win _____ blackjack.

14. My friend likes to bet _____ football games, and _____ times, he wins.

15. _____ time _____ time, I take a trip _____ a nice place _____ the world.

Prepositions 7

1. _____ my vacation _____ Italy, I spent time _____ my friend called Francesco.

2. When Francesco spoke _____ Italian, I was confused _____ what he was saying.

3. I am not talented _____ languages, so I need to work hard _____ learn a language.

4. If Canada was attacked _____ another country, I would fight _____ my country.

5. _____ wars, many people leave their homes _____ a hurry.

6. Lamps can light _____ a room, and light is needed _____ everyone.

7. Please get _____ the taxi. We are already late _____ the meeting _____ the boss.

8. When I dove _____ the pool, I swam _____ the pool to the other side.

9. _____ the last day _____ the year, people go _____ parties.

10. Asians eat _____ chopsticks, and usually share food _____ other people.

11. I have a beard, but I want to shave it _____. I look _____ a bear.

12. When I asked Hana to marry me, I knelt _____ the floor. She said yes _____ me.

13. If she said no, I would have jumped _____ this table, or cried _____ a year.

14. Red looks bad _____ me, so I never shop _____ red clothes.

15. Lights are _____ our heads, _____ the ceiling, and are made _____ glass.

Prepositions 8

Fill in the blank
Write a proper preposition for each sentence. Sometimes, there is more than one answer. Also, prepositions are used in Idioms. These phrasal verbs must be memorized.

1. Please sit _____ your chair, and take _____ your books.

2. Andy usually sits _____ _____ Susan.

3. The lights _____ this room are _____ students' heads.

4. The table is made _____ wood, and is _____ the window and the door.

5. If you are _____ an island, you should sit _____ a beach, and swim _____ water.

6. When I drive _____ my car, I always turn _____ the radio.

7. _____ my vacation, I will travel _____ Vancouver _____ airplane.

8. Air is _____ us, the sun is _____ us, worms are _____ us, and blood is _____ us.

9. Christine studies _____ 4pm _____ 5:30 _____ Monday.

10. The cat climbed _____ the tree, chasing _____ a squirrel.

11. Hey! Wait _____ me. I want to go _____ you.

12. I don't know, but I think I have _____ $20 _____ my pocket.

13. When you walk _____ a street, watch _____ for cars.

14. Paint is all _____ the walls.

15. I liked to walk _____ the St. Laurent River when I lived _____ Canada.

Prepositions 9

1. I came here _____ my friend _____ taxi.

2. My mom drops me _____ _____ school everyday.

3. What is exciting _____ your life_____ Montreal?

4. Are you happy _____ your life?

5. When did you get back _____ your trip _____ Spain?

6. Don't jump _____ the diving board _____ looking down.

7. If people dance _____ a long time, they will have pain _____ their feet.

8. What do you need that _____?

9. Please write _____ this paper _____ your vacation.

10. I am bored _____ my job. I have to look _____ another one.

11. I don't understand _____ all. I can't catch _____.

12. I got a discount _____ my car. I paid $10 000 _____ it.

13. Can you fit _____ these pants?

14. _____ water, plants die.

15. When she grows _____, she wants to make dresses _____ herself.

Prepositions 10

Fill in the blank
Write a proper preposition for each sentence. Sometimes, there is more than one answer. Also, prepositions are used in Idioms. These phrasal verbs must be memorized.

1. He arrived _____ Montreal _____ airplane.

2. He arrived _____ Dorval Airport _____ an airplane.

3. The cat walked _____ the chair and _____ my arms.

4. I have to go _____ the dentist _____ a check-up.

5. She will be _____ the hospital _____ 3pm.

6. I'm coming home _____ Thursday morning _____ my dog.

7. We are studying _____ the test.

8. We study _____ the 3rd floor _____ the building.

9. Please wait _____ me to go shopping _____ a coat.

10. Please wait _____ 2 o'clock. Then you should go shopping.

11. I haven't seen her _____ several days.

12. I've never seen such a beautiful day _____ all my life.

13. _____ the supermarket, I hate waiting _____ line.

14. When you walk _____ a path _____ a mountain, walk to the top _____ the mountain.

15. He studies _____ French, but he is bad _____ French.

Prepositions 11

1. Stop laughing _____ me or I'll pee _____ my pants.

2. I wouldn't want to live _____ a tiger.

3. Could you look _____ my fish while I am in the jungle?

4. I ran _____ a bottle _____ my car yesterday.

5. What does ASAP stand _____?

6. I could really go _____ a hamburger right now.

7. If you cancel something, you are calling it _____.

8. Please don't cut _____ that tree. Many birds live _____ it.

9. Please eat _____ all your potatoes. They are delicious.

10. Fill _____ the answer to this question.

11. Can you find _____ who broke my radio?

12. You must hand _____ your homework _____ Friday.

13. When robbers steal money _____ a bank, it is called a hold _____.

14. Please pass these papers _____ the class.

15. That boy is _____ grade 5.

Prepositions 12

Fill in the blank
Write a proper preposition for each sentence. Sometimes, there is more than one answer. Also, prepositions are used in Idioms. These phrasal verbs must be memorized.

1. There is a telephone call _____ you. She sounds _____ an old lady.

2. _____ dawn, _____ the afternoon, _____ dusk, _____ the evening,

    _____ night.

3. I was bad _____ soccer, but I played _____ a team last year.

4. The bad guy was put _____ jail _____ a bus, not _____ a car.

5. The cartoons _____ YTV are funny _____ me.

6. I was driving _____ a bridge when I saw an airplane _____ the sky.

7. He arrived _____ Vendome station _____ the morning.

8. The cat jumped _____ the table, and the floor.

9. I have to go _____ the dentist _____ a street _____ my home.

10. She is _____ the hospital right now.

11. I'm coming home _____ Thursday morning _____ my friend.

12. We have been studying _____ 10 o'clock _____ these books.

13. We have been studying _____ 2 hours _____ a test.

14. Please wait _____ me to go shopping. Don't go _____ yourself.

15. Please wait _____ 2 o'clock. Then you should go shopping.

Prepositions 13

1. I had a dream _____ my bed last night. I was flying _____ the earth.

2. I could see people walking _____ the Great Wall _____ China.

3. _____ the people, I could see a beautiful girl.

4. She was _____ to fall _____ the Wall.

5. A man started to run _____ her very quickly.

6. Many people started to gather _____ the two people.

7. There were 7 students sitting _____ the table.

8. _____ the class began, a knock was heard _____ the door.

9. One student was _____ to open the door when a man walked _____

10. He looked _____ the students, then put his coat _____ a chair.

11. The light _____ the strange man's head went _____.

12. His bag was _____ his chair. The people _____ the class were interested

13. He was the strangest person I have seen _____ my life.

14. I like it when the wind blows _____ the window.

15. Here's $10 _____ the book. Please give me _____ the change.

Prepositions 14

Fill in the blank
Write a proper preposition for each sentence. Sometimes, there is more than one answer. Also, prepositions are used in Idioms. These phrasal verbs must be memorized.

1. The sick person checked _____ the hospital.

2. This story is terrible. You must do it _____.

3. The bad student dropped _____ of school.

4. Can you figure _____ the answer _____ this question?

5. Do you get _____ with your neighbours?

6. I can't climb this mountain. I'm going to give _____.

7. If you don't know what the word means, look it _____ in your dictionary.

8. He drank so much water that he ran _____ the bathroom, and shut _____ the door.

9. What time should I show _____ for the meeting?

10. My sister really looks _____ my father.

11. Why don't you take _____ your coat.

12. Please throw _____ your old shoes.

13. I can't hear the radio. Turn it _____.

14. The rocket took _____ early _____ the morning.

15. I ate some bad food so I threw _____.

Prepositions 15

Fill in the blank
Write a proper preposition for each sentence. Sometimes, there is more than one answer. Also, prepositions are used in Idioms.
These phrasal verbs must be memorized.

1. Don't walk _____ a street _____ looking both ways first.

2. The sky is _____ our heads, and is filled _____ clouds.

3. _____ March, I went _____ vacation _____ my friend.

4. We study _____ a book made _____ Amy, your favourite teacher _____ the world.

5. There are some red books _____ the things _____ the table.

6. I walked _____ a river 3 years ago _____ Korea.

7. The chairs are _____ the table.

8. I think it is _____ to snow outside.

9. _____ the countries in Asia, I have not been _____ Vietnam.

10. Air is all _____ us.

11. _____the summer time, I like to lie _____ trees.

12. My sister is interested _____ studying _____ stars _____ the sky.

13. I always put a towel _____ me when I lie _____ the ground.

14. People _____ _____ _____ my home usually play games like basketball.

15. They try to throw a ball _____ a basket.

Articles Section

Articles 1

Fill in the blanks (a, an, the or X)
Articles are always used before nouns. Common singular nouns (i.e. a car, a chair, an apple) are the most common nouns to take articles. Proper nouns (i.e. The Hudson River) sometimes take the article THE, sometimes not. Non-counting nouns and plural nouns also take articles sometimes, if they are known to the speaker (i.e. The water in my glass is hot)

In _____ world, there are many strange _____ animals, and one of _____ strangest is

_____ bat. _____ bat eats mostly _____ bugs, so _____ people who live near _____

bats are usually very happy. _____ Bat is blind, and it sees by using its voice. _____ Bat lives in

_____ cave, like _____ Fregosi Caves in _____ Italy, and they live in _____ group, not

alone. One time, _____ bat came into my home, and my father was _____ angry man. That was

_____ first time I ever saw him so mad. He picked up _____ broom, and chased _____ bat for

half _____ hour. Finally, _____ bat flew out _____ window in _____ kitchen, and we all

felt _____ lot happier. _____ Bat is not _____ dangerous animal, but people are _____

little afraid of them. Some bats drink _____ blood. They are called vampire bats, but they cannot change

into _____ vampire, so don't worry. If you see _____ bat in _____ sky on _____ warm

summer night, remember that _____ bat isn't looking for you. In fact, _____ bat is more afraid of you

than you are of it.

Articles 2

_____ First time my family bought _____ TV, I was such _____ happy boy. It was _____

small TV, made by _____ Sony company, and it was made in _____ United States. It was _____

color TV, and my favorite channel was _____ CBC because I could watch _____ hockey game every

Saturday night. _____ TV changed _____ world _____ lot, especially my world, because I could

see _____ lives of people in _____ other countries. In _____ China, I saw _____ Yellow

River, and in _____ Republic of Korea, I saw _____ Namsan Tower and _____ Kyungbok Palace.

In Japan, I saw _____ Osaka Castle and _____ Fuji Mountain. In Africa, I saw _____ Pyramids in

_____ Egypt. In Europe, I watched _____ Rhine River, _____ London Bridge, and _____

Louvre Museum in _____ city of Paris. _____ Only problem with having _____ television was

that I stayed at _____ home too much. So, my mom threw _____ TV into _____ garbage after I

got _____ F on _____ Math test.

Articles 3

_____ First time I won _____ prize, it was _____ 1st prize in _____ singing contest. At

_____ first, I was such _____ shy guy because I had never sung in front of _____ people before.

_____ song I picked was called "Crying", and I knew all of _____ words to _____ song.

_____ contest was at _____ McCord Museum on _____ Sherbrooke Street on _____ 2nd

floor in _____ large hall. When I walked into _____ hall, there were hundreds of _____ people,

all sitting on _____ chairs, practicing _____ songs they were going to sing. I waited for 2 hours and

_____ half, then _____ man called my _____ name, and then I went onto _____ stage,

and sang _____ song. When I was finished, _____ people in _____ hall were all quiet. I thought

that they hated me, but I was wrong. They began to clap their hands, and for _____ long time, I was

standing on _____ stage, _____ very happy person. At _____ end of _____ day, I won

_____ contest. _____ Prize was _____ trip around _____ world. It is _____ only

time I have ever won _____ contest, so I think I was such _____ lucky man. _____ trip was

fantastic, and I saw many great things. _____ Next time there is _____ contest, I will try again.

Articles 4

1. Cartoons on _____ Disney Channel always make me laugh _____ lot.

2. _____ Toyohira River has _____ lots of water and _____ fish in it.

3. In ____ Canada, you can go to ____ Pacific Ocean, or ____ USA by ____ car.

4. I have _____ same _____ hat that you have.

5. He has _____ cold, so he went to _____ Montreal General Hospital.

6. _____ Ball hit me in _____ leg, and it hurt _____ little.

7. In _____ 1990s, many countries built _____ homes and _____ buildings.

8. When she goes to _____ school, she always brings her _____ lunch.

9. _____ Elephant is _____ largest land animal in _____ Africa.

10. _____ Police in Canada carry _____ guns in case of _____ emergency.

11. My uncle went into _____ army when he was _____ young man.

12. _____ French language is not easy to learn.

13. _____ French love to eat _____ bread, and drink _____ wine.

14. _____ Olympic Stadium is in front of _____ Olympic Park.

15. At _____ Cavendish Mall, there is _____ grocery store inside.

Articles 5

1. She is _____ only person in _____ class who has _____ pet tiger.

2. _____ Botanical Garden in _____ city of Montreal is beautiful.

3. _____ Granby Zoo is quite _____ large place with many _____ animals.

4. _____ Hyundai is _____ most powerful company from _____ Korea.

5. At _____ Hae oon Beach, you can find _____ Hyatt Hotel.

6. _____ Grand Canyon, in _____ USA, is _____ very long and deep.

7. _____ Champlain Bridge was built in _____ 1960s.

8. In _____ Jasper National Park, you can climb up _____ Logan Mountain.

9. My grandmother had _____ small home near _____ Lake MacGuilvery.

10. Many ants live in _____ Sahara Desert.

11. _____ television was _____ great invention.

12. _____ Ostrich puts its head in _____ ground when it is scared.

13. My friend bought _____ guitar for _____ lot of money.

14. However, he can't play _____ guitar at all.

15. If he practices _____ guitar, he will join _____ band called _____ Fishes.

Articles 6

1. _____ Last year, at _____ Christmas, he bought _____ nice gift for my mom.

2. _____ Next time I go to _____ Netherlands, I will visit _____ Van Gogh Canal.

3. We study on _____ 3rd floor in this _____ building.

4. _____ Most people like to drink coffee in _____ morning.

5. I like smart students _____ most.

6. _____ University of McGill is _____ best university in _____ Montreal.

7. _____ United Kingdom has 4 countries, including _____ Ireland.

8. _____ Place where I live is on _____ Benny Avenue.

9. When I cook in _____ kitchen in my home, I put on _____ old shirt.

10. At _____ night, I saw _____ cat climb up _____ tree.

11. I have _____ car. _____ car is old, so I want to buy _____ new car.

12. In _____ evening, I teach _____ class to students who go to _____ high school.

13. I call my mother once _____ week.

14. _____ Thompson family is _____ richest family in Canada.

15. _____ First time I went to _____ Inchon Airport, I was _____ tired man.

Articles 7

I am sure that in _____ future, _____ people will live on _____ moon. In _____ 1960s,

_____ rockets were flying into _____ space, taking _____ men from _____ United States

and _____ U.S.S.R. (which is now called _____ Russia) to _____ big rock in _____ sky.

_____ Biggest problem with _____ moon for _____ humans is that there is no _____ air.

So I think _____ first people who live there will have such _____ hard time. Some of _____

planets close to our planet in _____ Milky Way have many _____ moons, but we have _____

only one. _____ Long time ago, some people believed that _____ moon was made of _____

cheese, but of course that is _____ lie. _____ First time I saw _____ full moon was in

_____ Rocky Moun-tains. I was camping near _____ Lake Willow, and as soon as I saw _____

moon, I knew that it was _____ most beautiful thing I had seen in my life.

Articles 8

_____ Smith family is _____ very special family because every person in _____ family is

_____ genius. There are two reasons why _____ family is so smart. _____ First reason is that

they all drink _____ special juice. _____ Other reason is _____ family studies all _____

time, and they study _____ same things every day. One day, _____ father told his family, "Today I will

make _____ new machine that will help all _____ people clean their homes more _____ easily."

Later that night, in _____ secret room in _____ basement of _____ house, _____ father

screamed happily. When he came out of _____ room, he was holding _____ ugly, square box.

Everybody in _____ family laughed, but when _____ father put _____ box down, _____ box

began to move. It moved fast. Really fast. _____ strange light went all over _____ room, and then

_____ light went off. When _____ family looked around _____ room, they were shocked.

_____ room was so clean that it shined like _____ sun. However, there was _____ problem.

_____ Smith family's father was so smart that he forgot to take _____ shower, so he was very dirty

too. When _____ box cleaned _____ room, it also cleaned _____ father away. _____

Smith family's father was gone, and nobody has seen him since _____ day _____ father invented

_____ super cleaning box.

Articles 9

Fill in the blanks (a, an, the or X)
Articles are always used before nouns. Common singular nouns (i.e. a car, a chair, an apple) are the most common nouns to articles. Proper nouns (i.e. The Hudson River) sometimes take the article THE, sometimes not. Non-counting nouns and plural nouns also take articles sometimes, if they are known to the speaker (i.e. The water in my glass is hot)

1. I have _____ car, _____ small car, and I always drive on _____ Decarie Expressway.

2. _____ only time I lived on _____ peninsula was when I lived on _____ Korean Peninsula.

3. _____ Great Barrier Reef in _____ Australia is _____ beautiful.

4. I didn't go to _____ school today. Instead, I went to _____ Ji hyun Beach on _____ bicycle.

5. If I go hunting, I bring _____ gun, and _____ gun is big. I go to _____ Min seo Forest.

6. He had _____ picnic at _____ Benny Park, and _____ weather was great.

7. I had _____ job near _____ East Sea. I had to catch _____ fish in _____ boat.

8. _____ boat's name was _____ John, and _____ captain was _____ blind.

9. At _____ top of _____ Fuji Mountain, there is _____ lots of snow.

10. In _____ Ji seon Building, on _____ 1st floor, there is _____ only one bathroom.

11. In _____ United States, there are _____ many high towers, for example, _____ SES Tower.

12. _____ Tower is near _____ Statue of Liberty and was built in _____ 1990s.

13. In _____ Liberty Square, many Egyptians fought against _____ government and _____ army.

14. _____ largest animal in _____ world is _____ whale, and I saw _____ whale 1 year ago.

15. I have _____ TV and it is made by _____ Toshiba, _____ company from _____ Japan.

Articles 10

1. On _____ Canada Day, you should go to Ottawa by _____ car and visit _____ National Museum.

2. _____ Price to go into _____ museum is _____ little expensive, but it is _____ fun place to see.

3. I have _____ test tomorrow, and _____ another on _____ 3rd of April.

4. _____ Jazz festival happens in _____ summer, and is _____ more exciting than _____ Tulip festival.

5. You have _____ hour to eat _____ onion and _____ apple on _____ table in front of you.

6. In _____ space, you can see many great things like _____ Haley's comet and _____ moon.

7. In _____ universe, there are many galaxies like _____ Milky Way.

8. At _____ church I go to, there are _____ great deal of nice people, so I like to go to _____ church.

9. Some _____ people believe in _____ God, but _____ others don't.

10. When Columbus sailed _____ West, he brought many things with him, like _____ compass.

11. If you go to _____ Botanical Gardens, near _____ Olympic Stadium, bring _____ camera.

12. I see quite _____ few beggars in Montreal. I think _____ poor have _____ hard lives.

13. _____ Einstein family is _____ famous family, but _____ only because of Albert.

14. _____ Sahara Desert is one of _____ hottest places on _____ Earth.

15. _____ Boshivio Theater in _____ city of Moscow is _____ world's _____ best theater.

Articles 11

1. _____ Ice Age was _____ time when all _____ weather was cold.

2. People in _____ France are called _____ French, and people in _____ Netherlands are called _____ Dutch.

3. I had _____ great time in _____ Europe. I took _____ week holiday there.

4. I can't play _____ piano, but I can play _____ UNO _____ little.

5. On _____ Baffin Island in _____ north, _____ few people live there because of _____ cold.

6. _____ United Kingdom used to be _____ enormous empire that controlled much of _____ world.

7. However, that is in _____ past, and now, _____ England is not _____ super power anymore.

8. _____ LG Twins play in _____ KBO, and _____ team is _____ strong team.

9. If you get _____ 99% on _____ final test, I will buy you _____ ice-cream, _____ hat and _____ coffee.

10. What did you do _____ last weekend? _____ same as usual. I had _____ boring weekend.

11. When you come here, turn _____ right on _____ Cavendish. _____ building is on _____ right.

12. _____ hottest place on _____ earth is on _____ equator. If you go, bring _____ sunscreen.

13. _____ Most people in our class have _____ car, but one person has _____ bike.

14. When I went to _____ Grand Canyon, I met _____ alien who was flying in _____ UFO.

15. _____ Alien asked me to have _____ lunch with him. I had no _____ time, and I left in _____ hurry.

Articles 12

The Bird and the Worm

There once was _____ bird that was always looking for _____ food because _____ bird was always hungry. Some of _____ it's friends called him _____ pig, which was strange since _____ pig is _____ animal that doesn't eat _____ lot, but _____ other birds didn't know that. One day, _____ bird was searching for _____ food in _____ Amazon jungle when after _____ several hours, _____ bird saw _____ worm moving at _____ slow speed away from _____ Nile river. _____ bird loves worms, it is their _____ most precious snack, so when _____ bird saw _____ worm on _____ sand, it flew down like _____ rocket taking off at _____ Inchon airport, and landed right in front of _____ worm. Before _____ bird could eat _____ worm, _____ worm spoke in _____ deep voice. "Hello, Mr. Bird, my name is _____ King Kala _____ Great, and I am _____ most delicious worm in _____ universe. If you eat me, you will be _____ happier bird than any bird in _____ northern hemisphere." _____ bird was _____ bit confused. "But," said _____ worm, "if you don't eat me as _____ snack, then I will tell you _____ secret about _____ worms so incredible that you might not believe me in _____ least."

"Tell me _____ secret now...you have half _____ minute or you will be my _____ lunch."

"_____ secret is that I know where _____ Worm Kingdom is, and I can take you there if you make _____ promise to me not to eat me." _____ bird is not _____ very smart animal, so _____ bird agreed, picked up _____ worm gently, and flew into _____ sky. _____ worm said, "You must fly _____ fastest you can, over _____ Atlantic Ocean, past _____ Golden Bridge, beyond _____ Swiss Alps and across _____ Hudson Bay." _____ bird's stomach was empty, but still it flew and flew, and after _____ hours, _____ bird decided to take _____ rest on _____ Maui Island. Right away, _____ bird fell asleep in _____ tree, and _____ the worm started to crawl away. "I always wanted to visit _____ Hawaiian islands..."

Articles 13

Fill in the blanks (a, an, the or X)
Articles are always used before nouns. Common singular nouns (i.e. a car, a chair, an apple) are the most common nouns to take articles. Proper nouns (i.e. The Hudson River) sometimes take the article THE, sometimes not. Non-counting nouns and plural nouns also take articles sometimes, if they are known to the speaker (i.e. The water in my glass is hot)

The Alien

When I was _____ 8 year old boy, I went to _____ St. Bernard Elementary School, and in my class,

there was _____ girl who was different from _____ other students in _____ class in many ways.

She was as quiet as _____ wind, her eyes were shiny like _____ sun, and her hair was long like

_____ legs of _____ giraffe. She was _____ strange looking girl, but I was in _____ love

with her, so after _____ school, we would walk home together through _____ Camden Park along

_____ Drooly Street, past _____ baseball field, and finally to her home near _____ highway. She

never spoke _____ word to me when we walked, but she always had _____ enormous smile on her

face when we said goodbye. On _____ last day of school, I was _____ sad person because I knew I

wouldn't see her for _____ whole summer, so I decided to ask her _____ question. I said, "What are

you going to do in _____ summer time, and will you marry me?" _____ words spilled out of

my mouth, and before I could say _____ another word, she ran into her house and shut _____ door. I

was such _____ dumb boy, and I just stood there for half _____ hour, staring at _____ house.

Suddenly I heard _____ rumbling sound, _____ sound so loud I thought there was _____ an

airplane flying in my brain. I looked at _____ house, and it started to move, and then it took off into

_____ sky, into _____ space, into _____ universe. That was _____ first and _____

last time I have ever asked a girl to marry me. I am still _____ single, but I am now 13 years old, _____

teenager, so I have _____ plenty of time to meet _____ other girls.

Articles 14

Breakfast

In _____ morning, I always wake up earlier than _____ other people in my building because I have

_____ special job to do before _____ dawn: I must make _____ breakfast for _____

Queen Hana and _____ King Rex. They are _____ rulers of _____ house I live in, and if

_____ breakfast I cook is not delicious, they get angry at me for _____ long time. One time, I decided

to make _____ omelet and I put _____ ketchup on _____ plate, but I put _____ little too

much, so _____ queen threw _____ plate onto _____ floor and told me to get out of

_____ house. _____ another time, when _____ breakfast was late by _____ 2 minutes,

_____ king decided to call _____ police, and I was put in _____ jail. So I have _____ good

reason for waking up early. Today, I wanted to make _____ most fantastic breakfast ever, so I went to

_____ Loblobs to buy _____ ingredients for _____ kalamazoo. _____ kalamazoo is

_____ pancake with many things inside of it: _____ fish from _____ West Coast of Vancouver,

strawberries from _____ Turner Hill, _____ almonds from _____ Pearl Harbour, tomatoes from

_____ MacDonald's farm, and even coconuts from _____ Lennon Field. It took me _____ hour

and _____ half to make _____ only one kalamazoo, but _____ kalamazoo is big enough for

_____ 2 people, so I wasn't worried. When I was finished, I cleaned all of _____ dishes in _____

sink, set _____ table, and rang _____ bell to tell _____ king and queen that _____

breakfast was ready. I was sweating like _____ pig in _____ oven when, finally, _____ two

people finally walked into _____ dining room. _____ Queen Hana took _____ look at

_____ food on _____ table, yawned, and said, "This does not look delicious, so I am going back to

_____ bed. It looks like _____ dog food," but happily Rex sat down in _____ chair, and started

to eat _____ kalamazoo.

Articles 15

A Trip to New York

In _____ summer, I usually take _____ trip to _____ New York City by _____ car because there are _____ great deal of _____ things to do there. _____ City of New York is also called _____ Big Apple, but that is just _____ city's _____ nickname. I have been there _____ one time in _____ winter, but _____ summer is _____ more fun time because _____ weather is better. _____ problem in _____ summer is _____ city has _____ smell that is really bad, but after _____ few days, _____ smell is not so bad. In NY, I have done many exciting things, like taken _____ elevator to _____ top of _____ Empire State Building, but I didn't see _____ King Kong. I saw _____ musical called _____ Phantom of _____ Opera on _____ Broadway, but I slept for _____ short time. I went to watch _____ baseball game at _____ Yankee Stadium, where _____ New York Yankees played against _____ New York Mets. It was such _____ hot day that I drank _____ liter of water every _____ hour. I also went to _____ Woodbury Shopping Mall, and I bought quite _____ few things like _____ pants, _____ jacket, _____ soap, _____ sunglasses, and even _____ handbag. _____ restaurants in New York are excellent, but _____ prices are _____ little high. When I come back _____ home, I have to cross _____ border from _____ USA back into _____ Canada, and sometimes that is _____ scary thing. One time, _____ guard asked me to open _____ trunk of my _____ car, but after _____ five minute search, he told me to keep driving along _____ Trans-Canada Highway. _____ Best time to visit New York is in _____ fall, I think, because _____ trees look beautiful, and _____ drive is long, so it is nice to look at nice things on _____ long drive.

Debate Section

Debate topics

- Students should not take tests.

- It is better to eat at home than at a restaurant.

- Zoos should be closed.

- Mothers should not have jobs.

- Traveling by boat is better than traveling by airplane.

TOPIC 1

TOPIC 2

TOPIC 3

TOPIC 4

Making Perfect Questions

MPQ 1

For each sentence, write a question that answers it. For example, if the sentence is "I brush my teeth 3 times a day", the question could be "How often do you brush your teeth?". Many questions can be used for each sentence.

1. I'm not a girl.

2. When I was young, I wanted to be a taxi driver.

3. I'll open it.

4. Stop asking that question, and run.

5. Rain and pain.

6. I will never tell you that.

7. For nearly 2 years.

8. He might have fallen asleep.

9. I had eaten breakfast before I came here today.

10. Hippopotomonstrosesquipedaliophobia.

MPQ 2

For each sentence, write a question that answers it.

1. The concert was great.

_____

2. I paid $200 for 1 ticket. I was ripped off.

_____

3. The yellow pencil with the red eraser belongs to me.

_____

4. In winter.

_____

5. I usually take a nap around 2pm.

_____

6. I have no idea what to tell you.

_____

7. You need to buy the pink medicine.

_____

8. I can't because it looks gross.

_____

9. Yes! I finally figured it out.

_____

10. This is my least favourite class.

_____

MPQ 3

1. I almost never use my Wii.

2. Cats and flies.

3. My dog barks, so some people don't like him.

4. The test will finish in 5 minutes.

5. I don't like horror movies.

6. She is the only person not from Canada in this class.

7. I got up at 5am today, and started working.

8. My car needs an oil change, so I'm going to the garage today.

9. Always.

10. You're always asking me to do that.

MPQ 4

For each sentence, write a question that answers it.

1. I had a really nice trip.

2. How dare you ask me that!

3. No, they didn't.

4. It's the last one on the right.

5. It will only be on sale for one more day.

6. Since 9am.

7. He smells like he hasn't taken a bath for weeks.

8. He told me that he is sick.

9. She started flying two days ago.

10. I don't think anyone is driving the bus.

MPQ 5

1. I will meet my friend tonight at 7pm.

2. I bought bananas.

3. I did it because I had to.

4. I like the pink jacket.

5. Today is February 25.

6. Yes, I have.

7. I left because I was tired.

8. She's been studying since 8am.

9. The car with the broken window is mine.

10. I'll be here 10 minutes longer.

MPQ 6

For each sentence, write a question that answers it.

1. I came here as soon as I woke up.

2. He can't eat peanut butter.

3. I would rather play tennis.

4. It will take me 2 hours to make the cake.

5. Yes, I could.

6. I wrote that while I was on the bus.

7. I wouldn't like to go because it is too late.

8. I sometimes call my mom on Sunday.

9. No, I wouldn't.

10. The last time I met my friend was 3 weeks ago.

MPQ 7

1. He is a very nice guy.

2. I ate breakfast as soon as I got up today.

3. He might be sleeping right now.

4. It was rainy, so we stayed home.

5. I came here on foot.

6. I was meeting my friend yesterday at this time.

7. I don't have any plans tomorrow.

8. Let's leave in 5 minutes.

9. I want to watch a movie tonight.

10. I have worked for 5 years at this company.

MPQ 8

For each sentence, write a question that answers it.

1. The movie lasted 2 hours.

_____

2. I don't have any money.

_____

3. I will be doing my homework at that time.

_____

4. I have lived there for 2 years.

_____

5. I don't like it because it tastes bad.

_____

6. I want all of them.

_____

7. It will take me 1 hour to finish my homework.

_____

8. She drinks water everyday.

_____

9. No, I didn't.

_____

10. Not yet.

_____

Making Perfect Sentences

MPS 1

Write a sentence using each word.

always	
her	
go swimming	
almost always	
pushes	
usually	
often	
wears	
break	
every other	
off	
a snack	
teaches	
kisses	
fixes	

MPS 2

Write a sentence using each word.

occasionally	
pays	
shave	
seldom	
fruit	
food	
in May	
never	
cries	
sometimes	
carry	
Thailand	
vegetables	
rarely	
almost never	

MPS 3

Write a sentence using each word.

every day	
lately	
two days ago	
next week	
since 9am	
would	
should	
might	
right now	
last night at	
tonight at 10 pm	
for 3 hours	
once in my life	
could	
may	

MPS 4

Write a sentence using each word.

can	
had to	
above	
outside	
between	
meet	
knife	
chopsticks	
will	
must	
near	
in the middle	
meat	
spoon	
fork	

MPS 5

Write a sentence using each word.	
people	
while	
during	
a fish	
a dream	
pizza	
feet	
furniture	
even though	
when	
dice	
a calendar	
dream	
they	
them	

MPS 6

Write a sentence using each word.

money	
traffic	
a few	
a bar of	
a jar of	
round	
some	
every	
mail	
few	
plenty of	
a can of	
a tube of	
circle	
any	

MPS 7

Write a sentence using each word.

one of	
each	
all students	
together	
time	
don't	
would	
pen	
none of	
every one of	
all of the	
kind	
book	
will	
did	

MPS 8

have you	
simple	
artistic	
a couple of	
alike	
if I study	
if I were	
less	
did your	
willing	
able to	
ago	
look like	
if it rains	
if I stayed	

MPS 9

Write a sentence using each word.

enough	
explain	
often	
bee	
play	
popular	
zany	
nincompoop	
ever	
forget	
size	
past	
around	
last	
too much	

MPS 10

Write a sentence using each word.

hers	
forest	
as	
behind	
paid	
spoke	
may not be	
possibly	
no one	
modern	
back	
below	
flew	
took	
might have	

MPS 11

Write a sentence using each word.

wish	
lend	
sleep	
hit	
see	
forget	
ring	
fly	
hope	
give	
bring	
cut	
ride	
send	
leave	

MPS 12

Write a sentence using each word.

take	
get up	
hang	
begin	
lose	
kneel	
sting	
flee	
steal	
tear	
shut	
find	
hide	
spit	
leap	

MPS 13

Write a sentence using each word.

as soon as	
the next time	
the first time	
not able to	
friendly	
brand new	
Japanese	
most of	
the first time	
the last time	
at first	
supposed to	
high	
khaki	
rubber	

MPS 14

Write a sentence using each word.

my friend's	
introduced	
not as old as	
sour	
hardly	
fluently	
eventually	
at last	
buy	
interested	
sweet	
salty	
honestly	
suddenly	
on top	

MPS 15

Write a sentence using each word.

sigh	
fly	
moan	
uncontrollable	
sadly	
stuff	
inch	
practically	
experiment	
information	
exquisite	
port	
exhausted	
within	
drown	

MPS 16

earliest	
eventually	
exaggerate	
tireless	
cobra	
bored	
cross	
eyelash	
embarrass	
exactly	
expression	
end	
even	
other than	
envy	

MPS 17

	Write a sentence using each word.
unlike	
can't be	
vet	
unlikely	
had better	
roast	
drums	
flute	
vacation	
restless	
volume	
force	
in the future	
enemy	
hardest	

MPS 18

Write a sentence using each word.

instead of	
grin	
double	
worth	
beverage	
attractive	
through	
terrible at	
show up	
cart	
taken	
fact	
about	
intend	
care for	

MPS 19

Write a sentence using each word.

obtain	
nowadays	
free	
gloat	
nevertheless	
sip	
nearly	
iron	
patient	
return	
her	
neighbourly	
none of	
asleep	
ankle	

MPS 20

Write a sentence using each word.

only	
tacky	
manly	
on the other hand	
one another	
temper	
pessimistic	
rush	
oily	
cheesy	
ask him to	
outstanding	
suit	
often	
wimp	

Writing:
Short Stories

Short Story 1

THE WATCH

Short Story 2

RED FINGERS

Short Story 3

CHOPSTICKS

Short Story 4

GOING HOME

Short Story 5

THE MILLIONAIRE

Writing: Essays

Essay 1

STUDENTS SHOULD NOT TAKE TESTS.

Essay 2

IT IS BETTER TO EAT AT HOME THAN AT A RESTAURANT.

Essay 3

ZOOS SHOULD BE CLOSED.

Essay 4

MOTHERS SHOULD NOT HAVE JOBS.

Essay 5

COMPARE TRAVELING BY BOAT AND TRAVELING BY AIRPLANE.

Essay 6

WHAT ARE THE EFFECTS OF EATING HEALTHY FOOD.

Essay 7

WHAT IS GOOD AND BAD ABOUT STUDYING ON WEEKENDS.

Essay 8

STUDENTS SHOULD WEAR UNIFORMS.

Essay 9

WHAT IS GOOD AND BAD ABOUT LIVING IN YOUR CITY?

Essay 10

WHAT DON'T YOU LIKE ABOUT YOUR LIFE?

Appendix

LIST OF PREPOSITIONS

Prepositions are words that tells us about where something is, or when something happens. They are always used to talk about nouns, like **on** TV, **in** my hand, or **above** my head. Here is a list of common prepositions:

aboard	about	above	across	after	against
ahead of	all over	along	among	apart	around
as	at	away	away from	back	before
behind	below	beneath	between	beyond	by
close by	close to	despite	down	during	except
for	forward	from	In	in between	in front of
inside	into	like	Near	next to	of
off	on	on top of	opposite	outside	onto
over	out	out of	round	past	since
through	to	toward	towards	under	until
upon	up	with	within	without	

OSASCNM – THE ORDER OF ADJECTIVES

In English, you must use adjectives in the certain order in a sentence. You must not mix up the order of the adjectives. It is one of English grammar rules.

If you can remember OSASCNM, then you will know the order of adjectives.

<u>O</u> = Opinion, <u>S</u> = Size, <u>A</u> = Age, <u>S</u> = Shape, <u>C</u> = Colour, <u>N</u> = Nationality, <u>M</u> = Material

◎ I have a <u>nice</u>, <u>big</u>, <u>old</u>, <u>square</u>, <u>brown</u>, <u>Canadian</u>, <u>wooden</u> chair.
      O   S   A   S   C   N   M

× I have a <u>big</u>, <u>square</u>, <u>Canadian</u>, <u>old</u>, <u>brown</u>, <u>nice</u> <u>wooden</u> chair.
      S   S   N   A   C   O   M

Present	Past	P. Perfect	Present	Past	P. Perfect	Present	Past	P. Perfect
awake	awoke	awoken	Come	came	come	freeze	froze	frozen
be	was/were	been	Cost	cost	cost	get	got	gotten
bear	bore	born	Creep	crept	crept	give	gave	given
beat	beat	beat	Cut	cut	cut	go	went	gone
become	became	become	Deal	dealt	dealt	grind	ground	ground
begin	began	begun	Dig	dug	dug	grow	grew	grown
bend	bent	bent	dive	dived/dove	dived	hang	hung	hung
beset	beset	beset	Do	did	done	hear	heard	heard
bet	bet	bet	Draw	drew	drawn	hide	hid	hidden
bid	bid/bade	bid/bidden	dream dreamed/	dreamt dreamed/	dreamt	hit	hit	hit
bind	bound	bound	Drive	drove	driven	hold	held	held
bite	bit	bitten	Drink	drank	drunk	hurt	hurt	hurt
bleed	bled	bled	Eat	ate	eaten	keep	kept	kept
blow	blew	blown	Fall	fell	fallen	kneel	knelt	knelt
break	broke	broken	feed	fed	fed	knit	knit	knit
breed	bred	bred	feel	felt	felt	know	knew	know
bring	brought	brought	fight	fought	fought	lay	laid	laid
broadcast	broadcast	broadcast	find	found	found	lead	led	led
build	built	built	fit	fit	fit	leap leaped/	leapt leaped/	leapt
burn	Burned/burnt	burned/burnt	flee	fled	fled	learn learned/	learnt/Learned	/learnt
burst	burst	burst	fling	flung	flung	leave	left	left
buy	bought	bought	fly	flew	flown	lend	lent	lent
cast	cast	cast	forbid	forbade	forbidden	lie	lay	lain
catch	caught	caught	forget	forgot	forgotten	light	lighted/lit	lighted
choose	chose	chosen	forego	forewent	foregone	lose	lost	lost
			forgive	forgave	forgiven			

cling	clung	clung
mean	meant	meant
meet	met	met
misspell	misspelled/ misspelt	misspelled/ misspelt
mistake	mistook	mistaken
mow	mowed	mowed/ mown
overcome	overcame	overcome
overdo	overdid	overdone
overtake	overtook	overtaken
overthrow	overthrew	overthrown
pay	paid	paid
plead	pled	pled
prove	proved	proved/ proven
put	put	put
read	read	read
rid	rid	rid
ride	rode	ridden
ring	rang	rung
rise	rose	risen
run	ran	run
saw	sawed	sawed/ sawn
say	said	said
see	saw	seen
seek	sought	sought
sell	sold	sold
send	sent	sent

forsake	forsook	forsaken
sew	sewed/ sewn	sewed/ sewn
shake	shook	shaken
shave shaved	shaved/	shaven
shear	shore	shorn
shed	shed	shed
shine	shone	shone
shoe shoed	shoed/	shod
shoot	shot	shot
show showed	showed/	shown
shrink	shrank	shrunk
shut	shut	shut
sing	sang	sung
sink	sank	sunk
sit	sat	sat
sleep	slept	slept
slay	slew	slain
slide	slid	slid
sling	slung	slung
slit	slit	slit
smite	smote	smitten
sow sowed	sowed/	sown
speak	spoke	spoken
speed	sped	sped
spill	spilt	spilt

make	made	made
spend	spent	spent
spin	spun	spun
spit spit	/spat	spit
split	split	split
spread	spread	spread
spring sprang/	sprung	sprung
stand	stood	stood
steal	stole	stolen
stick	stuck	stuck
sting	stung	stung
stink	stank	stunk
stride	strode	stridden
string	strung	strung
strive	strove	striven
swear	swore	sworn
sweep	swept	swept
swell swelled	swelled/	swollen
swim	swam	swum
swing	swung	swung
take	took	taken
teach	taught	taught
tear	tore	torn
tell	told	told
think	thought	thought
thrive thrived/	throve	thrived

set	set	set	spilled/	spilled/		throw	threw	thrown
thrust	thrust	thrust	wed	wed	wed	withhold	withheld	withheld
tread	trod	trodden	weave	wove	woven	withstand	withstood	withstood
understand	understood	understood	weaved/	weaved/		wring	wrung	wrung
upset	upset	upset	weep	wept	wept	write	wrote	written
wake	woke	woken	wind	wound	wound			
wear	wore	worn	win	won	won			

Homework